Container Gardening

Container Gardening

Poems by
Ellen Steinbaum

CustomWords

© 2008 by Ellen Steinbaum

Published by CustomWords
P.O. Box 541106
Cincinnati, OH 45254-1106

ISBN: 9781934999301
LCCN: 2008937218

Poetry Editor: Kevin Walzer
Business Editor: Lori Jareo

Visit us on the web at www.custom-words.com

Acknowledgments

Grateful acknowledgment is made to the following publications in which some of these poems first appeared: *Bellevue Literary Review, Brandeis Women's Publication, The Christian Science Monitor, Fulcrum, Ibbetson Street, Journal of Modern Writing, Midstream, Riverrun, Poetry Soup, Prairie Schooner, Saint Ann's Review* and *Somerville News.*

Special thanks for the gifts of nurturing time and space offered by the Virginia Center for the Creative Arts and the Duxbury Women Writers and Artists House; and of love, encouragement, and good advice generously given by Claudine Bing, Susan Donnelly, Frances Godine, Adele Margolis, Marcia Melamed, Sheila Estrin Reich, Ottone Riccio, Joan Sloan, Erica Stern, and Bruce Weitzmon; for the memory of Carl, always at the heart; and for the radiant presence of Jim.

for

Cameron, Zach, Mia, Ryan

Judith, Meg, Deborah

Table of Contents

I. Gathering

standing at the shore..13
Gathering...14
One Photograph...16
Generation 18
Primordial Soup...19
Time Travel..20
Letter Home..22
The Question...24
Artifacts..25
History Lessons..26
shared space..28
Container Gardening...29
Housekeeping..30
Anniversary...31
driving home in snow..32
Distant Relation...33
heirloom...34
When the mariposas come...35
it was the world the whole 36

II Ever Since

The Most Beautiful Words..41
Lachrymal..42
ever since..44
Iceman..45
Record breaking snow..46
At the Time Exchange..47
Alternative Healing...48
Home is where...49
Norman Conquest..50
Uncertain Times...51
Coffee 52
mending..54
How We Become Ordinary...55
September..56
Fare..58

Fortune..59
controlled burn...60

III   The Boat from Irian Jaya
Small Accident..65
The Time Emporium...66
Rochambeau..67
A Different Year..68
The boat from Irian Jaya...................................69
Archival Items..70
Leaving Wishes...72
Charlie, moving to London...............................73
Adjustments...74
Order..75
spinning...76
this page has been intentionally left blank............77
Yesterday, the damp earth smell rising
        around us,..78
Havdalah Prayer...79
Petition..80
a new you...81
"the half-life of desire".....................................83
Zach in the Garden...85
Now begins the dailiness:.................................86

I

Gathering

standing at the shore

afterwards we will
look at it and say
this was when we still or
this was before
but then we will not be
at that same soft moment
grouped in pastel shirts
the children giddy with being
on the beach at nearly bedtime
digging their toes into the sand
wild to escape to the waves
get their clothes wet
looking back we may see
the messy instant of everyone
trying to be perfect or
we may see it
framed by then
glowing
that minute
when we did not know where
we would be looking back from

Gathering

Early morning early spring on
Duxbury Beach: we sweatered few
bend to the task, finding
the perfect rock, begin the

weigh, discard,
wait to be called,
listen for magic.
On shelled beaches, too,

we search for the unbroken
clam or whelk, fingernail pink, white,
craggy grey, recent confidante
of tides.

We add it to the bowl, the small
assortment on the desk and soon
we cannot tell which one
was Normandy, Nantucket,

Kiawah, Carmel, which
was from snorkeling, first baby's
first umbrella'd beach, vacation
afterwards alone.

Closing the apartment of my
last, my favorite aunt, I found
her treasure rocks and shells
in bowls, on windowsills,

their histories of where and
when and how now

melted into
ground and air.

I brought them on the day we
gathered at her stone. We each
chose one to leave and one to
slip into a pocket, carry home.

One Photograph

She will not become my mother for another thirty
        years.
Her husband waits a quarter century into her future
and with him the war, letters, wounds.
Their home is not yet built, the molecules
and minutes of rooms and days
hang in the air.

What is here at this moment is the child
with her sisters all in white eyelet dresses their
mother has sewn, each dress slightly different.
In front, the two youngest sit, hands clasped. She
and the eldest stand behind them. Maybe their mother
        sits
nearby, proudly urging them into easy expressions,
formal, not quite smiles.

The child who will be my mother is seven, maybe
        eight,
staring solemnly ahead, looking for some
wanted thing—not the simple hard longing for the
        birthday
bicycle or prize behind the glass for which small
        damp change is
counted and recounted, but for what
she cannot name.

What would warm her,
fill her like soup
will flicker always
out of reach.

All of that is unknown at the moment of the
photograph. At that instant, perhaps she is thinking
if she concentrates, watches hard enough
it will be there soon, maybe just after
the shutter clicks.

Generation

Receive
the secrets.
Trace
the path.

Apprentice
yourself to magic
and the skill
of making fire.

On moonless nights
reweave the stories
thread by thread:
begin to sing

for Ricky

Primordial Soup

The week is measured out in dozens
of fragile hemispheres discarded,
their contents separated   beaten.
In heavy bowls the mountain ranges rise.
With a mighty hand I whip them
until stiff but not dry.
With an outstretched arm I fold
their quick breath into the sturdy mix.

Sifting through yellowed recipes
I am surrounded by ghosts of
past and future
every generation
tasting fresh greens
flavored with salt,
teaching me the mix
of bitter with sweet
at this season of my
daughter's birth,
my father's death.

Vanished faces surface
like soft bubbles rising in the soup
as I puzzle the riddles of another spring
and wish next year to be
nowhere else
but here in my kitchen
surrounded
by chickens and eggs.

Time Travel

Just before New Haven
a stone wall beside the Amtrak rails
spills white dot flowers,
small moss cushions.
Hollow buildings
once noisy with turning out staplers,
smelted iron, fine platinum,
have broken windows now and
crumbling brick, bleed graffiti
from 30th Street to Back Bay.

I am leaving Philadelphia behind:
an apartment closed, silent,
empty, some furniture
given to Goodwill: the last
chairs from the last apartment
of the last of my three aunts.
I am the owner now
of paintings I know by heart,
china from family dinners in old photographs.
Scarves that fill my drawers
once dressed my dolls.

I am the heir of
books and vases,
the samovar brought
by my great-grandmother
who died as I was being born,
candlesticks and tablecloths
from all the trousseaus,

and pairs and pairs of
white kid gloves—
in every picture they are
wearing gloves
and hats, smiling my smile—
and I received the gifts
without a question.

The Metroliner snakes
through New York tunnels,
past thick Connecticut landscapes,
New London's tethered boats
and I am carried away from Philadelphia.
In a wooded instant twenty minutes south of Boston,
a doe watches over her fawn.

Letter Home

I love you forever
my father's letter tells her
for forty-nine pages,
from the troopship crossing the Atlantic
before they'd ever heard of Anzio.

He misses her, the letter says,
counting out days of boredom, seasickness,
and changing weather,
poker games played for matches
when cash and cigarettes ran out,
a Red Cross package—soap,
cards, a mystery book he traded away
for *The Rubaiyyat* a bunkmate didn't want.
He stood night watch and thought
of her. Don't forget the payment
for insurance, he says.

My mother waits at home with me,
waits for the letter he writes day by day
moving farther across the ravenous ocean.
She will get it in three months and
her fingers will smooth the Army stationery
to suede.

He will come home, stand
beside her in the photograph, leaning
on crutches, holding
me against the rough wool
of his jacket. He will sit
alone and listen to *Aïda*

and they will pick up their
interrupted lives. Years later,
she will show her grandchildren
a yellow envelope with
forty-nine wilted pages telling her

of shimmering sequins on the water,
the moonlight catching sudden phosphorescence,
the churned wake that stretched a silver trail.

The Question

You do not choose. This is the one you are
given, the one that will be yours always. This
will be the mote at the edge of your vision,
the lost puzzle piece, the rough tooth edge.
This is the question that will be the whisper
in your ear, the rhythm of your breathing.
The answer is in the locked drawer, the one
that has no key.

Artifacts

Only two dollars, the vendor said
holding his flea market treasure
to my half-turned back: a brass
birdcage I did not need or want.
Only a dollar. How could I resist
the bargain? For years the birdcage
rested on my kitchen counter,
philodendron threading through the bars.

When my Aunt Alice died
I brought home paintings, books,
tissue-papered nightgowns,
careful rolls of ribbon, Stella and
Frank's wedding matchbook,
"Feb. 16, 1952."

Who were Stella and Frank? Did
Alice know them? Did they
turn out to be "a perfect match"?
The details crumble away like the soft
edges of antique shop photographs,
the faces staring out beyond our shoulders
to where their stories used to be.

History Lessons

our days are scored
by the soft percussion of treadle
soprano whirr of unseen needle
whizzing through the cloth she guides

child of her child
I am a docile pet
sitting beside her watching

how in her hand
wonders take shape in familiar sizes
acrobat combinations
sleeve glimpsed in a store window
collar from a favorite dress
skirt she saw on someone
strolling on the Boardwalk
all the sleeves will hug me

careful of dropped pins
I follow her quietly
padding to her kitchen
the only place where milk tastes sweet
even if it spills
she smiles and

tells me stories
of my great-grandparents betrothed as infants
of herself transplanted bride
learning with her children
the honeysweet language of her new home

how she tried to sell her waistlong copper hair
so dazzling the wigmaker would not cut it
of a son dead
in a sudden illness
that kills no one anymore
later she would give me the earrings
she could not bear to wear
after her brightest jewel was gone

stories with the treadle marking time
stories I will tell my children
without the accompaniment
they will hear only the words

shared space

stacked at the upper right
official documents
stapled left-brain neat
corners fixed as one
edges scissor sharp
words precise as knives

crammed in a cubbyhole
notes in helter-skelter sizes
paper-clipped haphazardly
some nearly getting loose
the way I'd quickly tie my hair
and escaping wisps
would fall across my face
waiting for your hand
to brush them softly back

a wind could blow across this desk
wafting ghosts of murmurings
through the constant air
without disturbing the stapled papers
at the upper right
hardly ruffling the paper-clipped notes
inside the cubbyhole
and leaving not a sign
of yellowed pages
tied with satin ribbons
at the bottom of the drawer

Container Gardening

Geranium, hosta, coleus,
lantana: beginner's garden
pieced from advice and
no-fail nursery specials

planted in recipe soil—
made earth lugged home
in separate bags and
measured out on careful plastic.

Two stories up they settle into air,
sip water doled out by the cup,
dare not drip on
downstairs neighbors.

No chance rocks here or beneficial insects,
glass shards, arrowheads, no earthworms
crawl among these roots, no weeds invade
and partial shade is all I have to offer.

I place each plant precisely,
add fertilizer, make the rain,
note blossomings and witherings,
apply attention—plainest form of love.

Still, I feel no gift for this,
distrust each curling leaf,
know when I banish from this garden,
the fall from grace is mine.

Housekeeping

The shutters are being painted
from bright to linen white,
taken from their hinges this morning,
sent away. Now sunlight pours through bare panes,
the view wide and unadorned, and time is measured
        out
in differences: when the shutters return
the leaves outside will be orange perhaps,
 or gone.

It was like that, too, when the hospital
bed arrived. Ours
went into storage—
a friend's convenient basement—
returning when I slept alone.
It was the same time of year,
leaves starting slowly to flame and fall.

Anniversary

It will become
your history, but
first it is unnamed.
You pass it, do not see
it waits, has waited
from the first day.

And what if you could
mark it in advance
before an end or a beginning,
before you gave yourself
to what is doomed—though
what, of course, is not—

would you refuse the gift,
stay safe inside the pillar
like Lot's luckless nameless
wife, keep turning still
to what you knew?

driving home in snow

let it unfold in leisure nudging gently at the roots
of scenes faint scents of conversations blur together
as I'm in the car alone in the first small snow and now
a late December afternoon just west of Boston is a
       Vermont
night our fingers freezing as we unload the skis how
       later
the restaurant will smell of dry firewood wet wool
       don't
rush sit back it tells itself the untracked hill me
       following you
but slowly fearful of a fall and long cold wait for
       rescue but
nothing happened nothing large or tragic we slide in
       and
out of focus conversations hang like old clothes we
       could
slip back into how we drank red wine beside the fire
       dozed
together through one snowy afternoon each at a sofa
       end legs
beside legs books and reading glasses slipping from
       our hands
waking with the fire out the music off moon shining
       across
new snow

And what was it I wanted to remember from
the snow? That we were there? That you were?

Distant Relation

A woman in Brazil may
or may not be my cousin,
sends photographs would I please
see if anyone looks familiar
and there
on my screen on my desk
the Atlantic City beach bright behind them,
the tsar and his war decades in the past:
my grandparents,
looking at someone from Brazil
who holds a camera. A hemisphere away
the maybe cousin brings
fruit compote to
a family dinner, and

given the way things work,
the way that dust motes
float from place to place,
drift down around the world,
the silt on my spring windowsill
may have been in Montana just last month
or on a Chinese breeze a century ago
flown from the Sahara Kalahari
Minsk or Mainz or Patagonia in
the Middle Ages and
on some yet-to-be-imagined street
may brush the cheek of my
great-great-grandchild
or of someone in Brazil
taking a picture at the beach.

heirloom

Only two things that money can't buy
That's true love and homegrown tomatoes.
                                   Guy Clark

reach
into the tangle of leaves
breathe in the green
hold out your hand
be patient and
if the time is right
the weight
will drop into your palm

be patient
this is what was given
from the start
a promise of vines
profuse   heavy
with abundant and
imperfect fruit

break it open
no knife no plate
no polite slices
just break it open
bite into the deep
sunwarm
simple crimson
let the juice
run down your arm

When the mariposas come

they turn the air to beating
flame, so many you can hear them,
so many that together—each the weight
of a hair—they bend the branches of the oyamel trees
in the cool high forests. It is the Day of the Dead
       when they
arrive, nearly spring when they cascade down from the
trees, begin the journey north. Four, five generations
die, are born along the way, ride on thermal
drafts and stars, return to where
they've never been.

When our cousin Eliana found us in her
online search, we were in Boston, Palo Alto,
Washington, New York, unaware of her in
Rio, Edgar in Moscow, Valentin in Tel Aviv,
but still carrying the impulse for ingathering,
quick to knit continents together, though lacking
bred-in-bone direction.

The old names circle back. We clutch our half-
remembered phrases, names of towns, draw
diagrams our children may yet read. We have
forgotten words and tune, but still the rhythm
runs unbidden in our veins.

it was the world the whole

world
hanging large and red
over the Boardwalk
lights blinking their way
down its curve
Sherwin-Williams paints
cover the earth

cover the earth
in glittering lights
in magic blinking childhood lights
a kind of Sherwin-Williams
grace a Sherwin-Williams
blessedness
blinking down the curve
of the world
blinking down to
cover the earth

cover the earth in blinking lights
in fine white sand
in bluewhite sandcrabs
sofa cushions
outdoor concerts

cover the earth in
rainy mornings
hot soup heavy quilts
scent of geranium leaves
ripe pears sliced on flowered china plates
Charms candy in my grandmother's handbag the war
          over and my father coming home

and all the brilliant vibrant shimmering
colors emerald scarlet midnight blue
vermilion topaz saffron every every color pouring out
to cover the earth
cover the earth
in flowers the drawings of children pied horses
Bengal tigers giant
redwoods
sparkling
fish

cover the earth
cover the earth

II

Ever Since

The Most Beautiful Words

Summer afternoon is the easy choice,
sound and sense murmuring together,
heat-stunned and slow. Harder would be
famine, assassin, carcinoma,
the way that, if you didn't know,
Manzanar could be a fragrant blossom
opening in moonlight, or
a lush island set in turquoise water;
Shiloh soft and whispering,
a meadow of tall grasses and fast wind;
Guantanamo a dance,
all jaunty hips and
flirting shoulders;
Gallipoli, Corregidor, Tonkin: exotic spices
men would sail for months to find.

Lachrymal

I.

The quality of your tears
has diminished, he tells me,

sliding back from
examining. I fear

this could be true.
Explaining drops and dryness,

the functioning of glands, he
says the tears have lost

viscosity,
break up. My old tears,

yes, were weightier,
purer, undiluted. They

could last for-
ever then.

II.

In Rome the women wore their tears
in tiny ribboned vials around their necks.

How in the rush of crying did they think
to press the small containers to their cheeks,

tears spilling through their fingers, and which tears, of
joy or sorrow, were more worth the gathering?

Were they storing up the old diverted tears
for keepsakes to remind them they had wept
as once again the men marched off to
war? Later, hardened to new grief,

they may have craved the blur
watching the crumbling begin.

ever since

now
in the fragile time
between the thunder claps
in the time after
the sky split open
and solidness
dissolved

the fire
continues
to leave no one
unscorched
shelter collapses
again and again
around us
the acrid dust
preserves us
perfect as Pompeii

we were gentle
with each other then
liable to break
now we sort through
what is left to us
sift the rubble
for what
we have lost

Iceman

He may have bled to death
there on the mountain:
flint arrowhead imbedded
in carbon-dated
shoulder blade, neolithic
agony echoing down to us
through tectonic shifts,
his computer image
looking like someone
I might have met.

I thought of him again—
I don't know why—
on a warm afternoon
later that September.

The streets were hushed and
shadowy although the sky,
of course, was emptier,
bluer, too, than necessary,
the scent still in the air and
flowers wilting
outside the fire stations,
posters in every window—
someone might yet come home.

In another age
a week before
we had owned small fears,
certainty.
We were young then.

Record breaking snow

obliterates a century.
Cars buried, the streets become
museum scenes in the flurried
streetlight, sound muffled,
time slow.

But inside our bright
rooms, we are online, e-
mailing, phoning at the very least.
No snow drifts cut us off from
miles-away prairie neighbors, leaving us
abandoned to our own
wits and muscle. We are
stoking fires, sleeping
under down while plows
scrape pavement through the night.

Next morning, squinting in the glare, we
carry our soft dogs to walking paths,
find the market ripe with peaches, wrapped
meats, still far from sell-by dates. Hot water rains
on us, we crank the heat, grind decaf French roast.
The paper, only slightly late, plops
on the doorstep.

At the Time Exchange

Picture them: the old
whose every waking is
a disappointment; the sad;
the sick wishing they could
slip off dreaming, peacefully sleep
away the grey remaining days..
At any given moment there are
those praying to die, and also

those praying to live: the ones with
weddings, impending births, precariously set
against the stage IV newly found,
tsunami, fire, skidding bicycle—
hands grasping out for
more. Imagine

they could
trade their fates—
days that,
unweighted,
drop away
or fall into their waiting,
grateful palms.

In any rational world
it would be like this.

Alternative Healing

The chi gong master
waves his hands above the spasms
that bend you in half while you
lie on a table, marionette on invisible strings.
Half a year's doctors found nothing;
half a year's x-rays, scans all normal,
but he knows your problem: chi is stuck, the pulsing
force of you frozen like a late leaf caught in a winter
stream.
                          With his energy,
without a touch, he frees it,
lets it course unbounded through an ancient mesh
of channels no ultrasound can find.
                          He knows the map
of person within person does not lie: we are not all
          blood
and bone. We hold mysteries surgeons cannot
          dissect,
reason cannot prove—how we breathe
when we forget to breathe, how a heart can squeeze
dry like a sponge and not lose rhythm.
                          You feel the heat
of his hands that write your body on the air, melt your pain,
never touch you. He says now you are well,
everything in balance. You rise, stand straight,
eat a lunch of foods
you have craved for months.

Home is where

the flowered field is plush
and comfortable as slippers
so we almost cannot see
hollow bones of fossil conversations
fill furrows that we flew across
before the land was mined.

Ghosts of words
cling to low scrub branches
and whisper with the wind
as we sit unruffled
in our fireside chairs
and read our books
and never think of when
the dry stiff grass
that bites our feet like tiny teeth
was soft and green.

Norman Conquest

See, on the granite column
the names and ranks are carved
on all four sides
and at its base a small
bouquet lies wet in rain
just like the rain
of sixty years ago.

Take care— the grass is slick
with rain and sea mist.
The hill is steep and rocky.
Everywhere you step
someone has died

And do you think it rained
the day nine hundred years ago
when William left
this hilly coast to conquer?
The tapestry unfolds
with the daring rush
of eager men and horses.

And see now the sun is out,
the raindrops steam up to the sky.
It may rain again tomorrow

Uncertain Times

Today I gave the cat my dinner,
tossed out the newspapers
all unread, ignored the ringing phone. I wore
one black glove,
one brown, kept the brown hand in my
pocket, pictured phantom
kisses growing
like a hedge between us in the bed.
I scrubbed the kitchen floor:
it's shiny now,
except for where I stepped with
muddy shoes. I hummed
a tune I didn't know. The dishes
are put away where I'll never
find them. All tidy now,
my coat on the
bookshelf, shoes
in the refrigerator. I'll
sit and listen to the walls.

Coffee

I measure out
the spoon of sugar,
scoop of powder
silken as breath,
stir the mixture on the stove,
its thick smell
already rising.

I am making coffee
in my new pot that is either
an ibrik or an imrik.
I may be making s'rj or kahve
in a cezva or a jesveh—
hard to say.

The choreography's precise,
identical no matter what the tongue:
dark roiling to the top,
three times the charm,
careful not to let it boil over,
this sweet and bitter drink
with many names, with none.

This perfect cup, owned
by each armed square of land,
holds the scent of scimitars and
cardamom, dust and blood.

Turkish, Armenian,
Armenian, Turkish,
minefield of an order,
could as well be Arab and

Israeli, English and Irish,
Bosnian and Serb, Moabite
and Midianite. You can read
your fortune in the grounds.

mending

what is broken can
            (never)
be repaired
the pieces can
            (not)
be put back
shift them beneath your fingers
without looking
feel the jagged tender shards seek
their place
turn them
let them catch the light
hear them singing in your hands
take them all
each hair each blink
each ineffable leaf
find the most sacred fit
for the rough shining edges
it will be
            (almost)
like new

How We Become Ordinary

It starts in such small ways:
how, when her hair is pulled back,
bright strands falling on her face
as she bathes the tiny child,
he asks what's for dinner,
leaves jars on the kitchen counter
with their tops off.

They begin the microscopic
calibration of words,
measuring of let-out breath,
backing away from the sharp risk
of losing fragile balance.

She will sit, furious, in the car
counting minutes and days,
while up in his
important office,
he takes longer than he said,
not seeing how

she waits in her
small insistent world,
handing crackers to the child in his
car seat who pushes each into his mouth
with his innocent palm and
reaches out again.

September

Spattered recipes line the kitchen counter. I roll bits
        of dough smooth
between my palms, drop them into bubbling gingered
        honey.

The birthday of the world returns: we wait to be
        inscribed
for life, for death, by strangling, by stoning, by fire, by
        water.

The children wear new shoes. Their notebook pages
        are blank.
Beneath the warm air, sweet with apples,

the faint chill breathes and waits. The sky is clear—
a shining blue, clear and innocent beyond naming—as
        we move through

calendar turns of ruined temples, vapored cities and
        time, as well, of
births and weddings, miracles, horrors in relentless
        patchwork. On one

September day we watched the sky darken with
        smoke and the slow
motion folding down to dust. In a different year

I drink strong coffee at the kitchen window, my face
        turned to the sun while,
elsewhere waters fall and rise as if the world will start
        again.

I mound the honeyed pieces on my mother's cut glass
        platter,
mark private harvests, losses on the page.

Red flames into ruby, green deepens to emerald,
        turning, turning,
in jeweled preparation for white sleep while

September gathers us in without mercy,
breaks us open once again.

Fare

Putting away the
dinner leftovers
tuned in to the news,
I wrap ripe cheeses,
toss the crackers.
scrape bones and scraps.

On camera
dirt cakes bake
in the African sun.
Outside a neighbor
tosses biscuits to his
two Jack Russells.

Across an ocean a woman
uses meager wood,
boils stones in a pot,
tells the crying children
go to sleep,
soup will be ready soon.

Fortune

Deafening jackhammer echoes sound
through the garage, ricochet off concrete
as I walk to my car. In some other place or
even here some other day, the repair sounds
could make me fly for cover, shield
my face from raining glass. But I
am blessed, swaddled in a place of
bags bulging with ripe fruit, fresh meats,
no insects buzzing at my children's eyes.

From the beginning the question is
the end, the answer, faint and personal,
already visible in the nursery nightlight
throwing tall shadows on the wall
behind the crib: who learns to crouch,
breath held, at sudden sound, who takes
for granted a garage might need loud
repair, whose shining food is cut
to size by unseen hands, who is
born to scratch at barren earth,

controlled burn

she is always preparing
to vacate his life
searching for the hint
in the message replayed
weighing the style and substance
of the invitational kiss

she is armed   he is dangerous
the ending that waits for them
will grow from his life
like a sudden mushroom
she will not see it coming

she feels dizzy
real though metaphoric
she is inventing boundaries
spending leisure hours
meticulously building walls
between yes and goodbye

this was always
temporary
one foot in the water
sealed lips
and wary secrets

she wants
to invent a signal
a tug on the earlobe
subtle quirking of eyebrow
would be all she'd need

freeing
how catastrophe inoculates
emboldens her now
to open umbrellas
in the house

in the night the covers creep
to the side where
no one sleeps
how that happens
is unclear

III

The Boat from Irian Jaya

Small Accident

The fall was fast and
innocent; nothing sharp
or speeding was involved, no
great harm—his lip, her

scraped knee. She
tripped, he was in front,
they both went down. A
blink, then it was over.

By morning it will be almost
fine, but now he tongues
the swollenness beneath
the ice cube. "You pushed me

down," he says. No tears, no
accusation: just the facts and
small surprise while she
swallows down the thickness

in her throat. "You're
supposed to protect
me. You're
my mother."

The Time Emporium

And which was your favorite
bauble—the perfect summer evening,
sky just darkening amethyst,
a scattering of fireflies for props?
Or maybe the birthday
when you were six, everyone
close around you singing, you
feeling beloved and fortunate?
The child's birth, first heart-stopping
smile, cheeks pink and damp from
sleep? The love, the passion,
intimate exchange, secret look in
the offhand moment? What was
that instant when you soared beyond
your skin, felt your benevolent soul
stretch outward? Which trinket catches
light, which jewel is bright with fire?
Which, looking back, would you never
exchange for what was coming next?

Rochambeau

Looking back I'd
have to say that I was
scissors,
you were
rock,
though no real
breakage was involved and
things played back and forth quite
evenly, you just the
slightest bit ahead, and
through the years the
scissors
(edges eased to
harmlessness) and the tranquil
rock
reposed in amity while
something we did not yet know
was
paper.

A Different Year

There was a summer solstice when
the sweet air held me in its palm,
the heat annealed me, left me gleaming.
I arose and opened to the sun, stretched out
into the long-lit day.

Now, years later, I feel the loss of every
daylight minute. For three nights my dreams
were filled with insects: in drawers of old letters,
roach-colored wings sheer between thick cream pages;
a swarm of flies above a truck piled high with toys,
some outgrown and others not yet
opened, a pale worm making its wrinkled way
back beneath the grass.

The boat from Irian Jaya

never came. If it had
he would not have taken
the flight to Kuching
where he met the man
who spoke to him of Langkawi
where he saw the photograph
that drew him to Alor Star
where he met the woman
who came home with him to Boston
where they bought the house
where they raised the children
who would have been
different children
in a different house
if the boat from Irian Jaya
had arrived.

Archival Items

It falls from the book
you bought for
in-flight reading.

> *on July 29 American 407 you sat in 14F non-*
> *smoking that's how long ago it was going from*
> *Houston to San Fran*

I'm clearing bookshelves,
lightening my hoard of things
before it falls to someone else
to do the culling.

> *Pan Am 4807, Logan to JFK,*
> *Nov. 9, seat 20A*

I am moving to new
bookshelves, new walls,
sifting through
artifacts of

> *VASP 268, Feb. 2, noon*

extinct airlines,
extinct rooms,

> *Pan Am Laguardia-Miami, Oct. 27*
> *3E, gate 19*

antique tickets to
time and place you spent

without me
falling to the floor.

Varig 110, 11/4, seat 3C, gate 1

I could toss them, the logical
thing to do. I could toss them,
but I don't. I clip them

PanAm JFK to Rio, March 4

together,

TransBrasil 505, 6/3, SSA to GIG

label a folder,
"things I cannot throw away."

Leaving Wishes

It's not the Western Wall,
urgent wishes on a thousand
bits of paper in the shadowed spaces
between the sunwarmed stones.

No, I'm in Philadelphia,
alone as the restaurant begins to fill,
next to me a space in the exposed
brick wall and, deep between the bricks,
a paper, yellowed, folded small.
I tease it out, open it: it is blank.
And I, who cannot leave a star
unwished on, write one small word,
retrace the paper's folds,
replace it in its niche, brush the
salting of brick dust from the
tablecloth, and wonder who
would have missed the chance
to wish, or could not trust
a wish to solid writing.

Then I see the wall is peppered with
openings, each big enough to hold
a wish. I could have wished again,
again, given some away. There are
clefts enough for everyone, the couple
reaching hands across the table,
the friends leaned in and whispering—
everyone around me talking, eating, unaware
they were so close to all that they could wish for.

Charlie, moving to London

We know the stories:
wagons lumbering slowly westward,
families remaining east forever
and the steerage bags holding
mismatched candlesticks,
exchanged by friends
parting for life,
the journeys always perilous
and to uncertain destinations.

In the third millennium, goodbyes,
like everything, are swift and temporary—
our ties wired into place
with digital pictures on the desktop
conveying all but touch,
e-mail oblivious to time zones,
airplanes gliding easily between us
on elastic paths.

What remains in place
is our constant effort
of desperate not seeing
how we spend each minute
leaving the one before,
how free will comes down to this—
grasping the present instant
until it sifts
through our clenched fingers
or hurling ourselves
into the next mutating second
as if the choice is ours.

Adjustments

"I cut a piece of brown paper
the size of the picture," she
tells her companion at the
table next to mine. "Then I
tape it to the wall, move it to find
the right place. How else
can you hang a picture
when you live alone?"

I sip my tea, think of the antique lace blouse
bought on a drizzly day along the Loire. I
held it to my raincoat, gambled on the size,
handed over crazy francs, wore it often,
sleeve ends ruffled on my wrists. He
would fumble with the covered buttons
down the back, high collar to peplum waist.

Afterwards, I wore it once,
knocking on a neighbor's door
for buttoning. In the bathroom
after dinner, a friend undid
the back. I drove home with
the blouse drooping loose
beneath my coat.

Order

I always know where
the tape measure is now,
a pen, a safety pin, my keys.
Not like the years when
shoes tumbled uncoupled
on the floor and every closet
could spill secrets.

Now each day is folded,
neatly stacked in silent drawers
and nothing moves an inch
to left or right.
In an instant I can find
the tape measure.

spinning

even now
all these years later
it can catch me
offguard
the phone rings
or a thought
brief as a blink
comes to me
and I turn to you
out of long instinct

in the non-you present
neat stacks of weekly
magazines and daily papers
slip into disorder
unread un-understood
each thing flies off
in its own direction

spinning
uncontrolled but
slowly
sliding
melting
falling away
nothing actually spins
except the universe

this page has been intentionally left blank

its emptiness echoing
the convalescent heart
now bare of flush
and flutter

choosing what is
over what might be
enduring the unchosen
anyway

desperate only for
no change
good or bad
makes no difference

makes no difference
fill it with the dinner
party menu random addresses
groceries to buy

try never to consider
what might have been written
what you might have said
instead

Yesterday, the damp earth smell rising around us,

we mounded up the ground,
breaking the hard clods with our fingers
to sift them gently down.
(How you would have loved
that all our backs bore
muddy evidence of hugging.)
Today we wake alone, resume
irrelevant breathing,

recognizing even the best end badly—
leaving, being left—
the difference merely temporary.
Lemmings, we run
to what destroys us,
condemned to give our hearts
to what is mortal.

We guard ourselves,
hunch-shouldered,
against the heavy sunlight,
hard-wired to crave the touch
that burns us every time,
the choice resting
in our own wounded arms—
hold back: we dry and shrivel
embrace: we are undone.

for Jason

Havdalah Prayer

as the sky darkens
as the moon appears
let the softness stay

make me like a pear
let me never harden
against touch

even if I bruise
send me out into the dusk
tender   undefended

scented flesh and juice
carrying the seed
sweet and secret flame

Petition

My daughters know anything can happen.
Holding their babies close, they tell me
stories they have heard: neighbor children
burned in their colorful beds, struck down in
driveways by their parents' shining cars, or,
from far away, other unthinkable shrugging-off
the trifling weight of their only lives:

murdered by marauders while tending goats,
caught between bullets on an unblessed street.
And it does not end, of course, as the mothers
of soldiers always know; the everpresent
scythe is sharp to cut down what we love.
I have no wisdom here, no rights, no hard experience
gained through famine or bad luck.

My ancestors were loath to tempt
the evil eye. Poo, poo, poo, they spat,
refused to praise too much lest the angel
of death covet their prize, knowing all the while
the ruse had doubtful value. I desperately
rejoice at minor colds, small naughtiness.
No, we have no perfection here—see
this tiny blemish, this one is a picky eater,
that one sleeps poorly, pouts sometimes.
No jewels for your crown here, dark angel.
Not one is unflawed: pass them by.

a new you

imagine the floor
sliding away
fast   slow
makes no difference
changing every minute
new surface replacing it
inch by inch
your feet tripping backwards
every shirt in your closet
unfamiliar
refrigerator filled
with someone else's meals

imagine your hair longer
curling   straight
imagine yourself
taller   shorter
deeper voiced
whatever wasn't

from every city
news of disasters gathers
in your room
gouge an amulet nick
in the furniture

imagine you imagine
new blood flowing
through your strange arms
words congealed
so thick you can barely

swim through them
barely come up for air
barely reach down
to tie your
new shoes

"the half-life of desire"

that's what Mike Fisch said
on Public Radio
I used my Visa card
to order the transcript
just to hold those knife-edge words
to look at them in wonder
and try to remember
when desire was a whole
and breathing thing
warm against my neck

there was something
about a mango
its juice dripping down the page
licking my lips
whispering of when the slightest
thought was enough
to hollow my stomach
with a swift squeeze
whispering of music
tangled and dappled as wild vines
and of dances I dance
only in dreams

I seldom see the ocean
though I live nearby
I look across the river
at a landscaped shore
pretend it is enough
pretend its small breeze
is breath enough

and turn away from the off-chance
of the squeeze that could be
peril or nirvana

but the lost atoms search for me
they creep beneath my shirt
the ripe mouth of desire
hot and open on my skin
as I edge my finger tentatively
along the risky blade

Zach in the Garden

I show him the pot of herbs,
tell him he can try any of these
leaves, forbid the rest. He picks
and tastes, eats mint, basil, parsley;
spits out tarragon and thyme; he sniffs
geranium, strokes furred lambs' ears,
pours water on dicentra. Soon
I will show him how
to deadhead.

Now begins the dailiness:

more days, if we are lucky,
than we will think to count,
piling up like shelter
at our door.
Feathered twigs and bits of string
will weave day upon day
and we will lean unthinking
on this solidness,
rest within the wonder
of this gift.

for Deborah and Michael

Ellen Steinbaum is the author of the poetry collection, *Afterwords,* and a one-woman play, *CenterPiece.* She writes a literary column for *The Boston Globe.* Originally from Wilmington, Delaware, she now lives in Boston. Her work can be seen at ellensteinbaum.com.

This book is set in Garamond, one of a group of old-style serif typefaces named for Claude Garamond (1480-1561). Garamond was regarded as the best typecutter of his day and the Garamond letterforms are known for their sense of fluidity. The only complete set of the original Garamond dies and matrices is at the Plantin-Moretus Museum in Antwerp.

CPSIA information can be obtained at www.ICGtesting.com
Printed in the USA
BVOW011641080212

282464BV00003B/389/P